Children's Authors

Avi

Jill C. Wheeler

ABDO Publishing Company

visit us at
www.abdopublishing.com

Published by ABDO Publishing Company, 8000 West 78th Street, Edina, Minnesota 55439.
Copyright © 2009 by Abdo Consulting Group, Inc. International copyrights reserved in all
countries. No part of this book may be reproduced in any form without written permission from the
publisher. The Checkerboard Library™ is a trademark and logo of ABDO Publishing Company.

Printed in the United States.

Cover Photo: AP Images
Interior Photos: AP Images pp. 5, 7, 13, 17, 21; Getty Images pp. 9, 11; iStockphoto
    pp. 15, 19

Editors: Tamara L. Britton, Megan M. Gunderson
Art Direction: Neil Klinepier

Library of Congress Cataloging-in-Publication Data

Wheeler, Jill C., 1964-
 Avi / Jill C. Wheeler.
     p. cm. -- (Children's authors)
 Includes bibliographical references and index.
 ISBN 978-1-60453-075-9
 1. Avi, 1937---Juvenile literature. 2. Authors, American--20th century--Biography--Juvenile
literature. 3. Children's stories--Authorship--Juvenile literature. I. Title.

 PS3551.V5Z95 2009
 813'.54--dc22
 [B]
                                        2008004800

Contents

Meet Avi

Over the years, Avi has written a little of everything. He has written books for children and young adults. There have been funny stories, dramatic tales, and science fiction and fantasy books. However, Avi is best known for historical fiction.

Many fans admire Avi's work because he explores what it is like to be an outsider. He also writes about young people who take on unjust situations and work to fix them. The experiences make the characters wiser and stronger.

Avi grew up in a family of **activists**. His work reflects his lifelong interest in equality and human rights. Avi says he likes to write about **complex** issues. Yet, he does so in a way that captures and holds a reader's attention.

Writing is a time-consuming process for Avi. He may rewrite a book 50 or 60 times! Each time he rewrites, Avi says he sees things he did not see before. Avi once said he would be satisfied having six books published in his lifetime. He has now written more than 50.

Opposite page: *When the publisher asked how Avi wanted his name to appear in his first book, he said, "Just put Avi down."*

A Family of Artists

Avi was born Edward Irving Wortis on December 23, 1937, in Manhattan, New York. He had a twin sister named Emily. Emily began calling her brother Avi because she could not say his real name. Soon, the rest of the family called him Avi, too.

Avi and Emily's father, Joseph, was a **psychiatrist**. Their mother, Helen, was a **social worker**. They also had an older brother named Henry.

Avi and Emily were the newest members of a creative, talented family. One of their great-grandfathers was a professional storyteller and singer. Another great-grandfather was a writer. A grandmother had written plays. An aunt was a journalist, and two uncles were painters. Avi's parents wrote books and articles related to their jobs.

With this background, it is no surprise that Avi grew up hearing stories. His mother also read to him a lot. Their home was filled with books. Avi also spent many hours listening to **serials** on the radio.

According to family legend, Avi taught himself to read. One night, five-year-old Avi ran up to the dinner table. He proudly announced that he could read!

Avi went on to read almost anything he could find. He liked stories about animals. He also read adventure stories and mysteries.

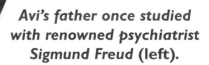

Avi's father once studied with renowned psychiatrist Sigmund Freud (left).

Struggles at School

Avi grew up in Brooklyn, New York. There, he went to elementary school at Public School 8. When Avi started school, America was fighting **World War II**. He later wrote a book about a young boy during the war. The book is called *Who Was That Masked Man, Anyway?* Many things mentioned in the book happened to Avi in real life.

Avi struggled with his schoolwork. He might write the same word three times and spell it differently each time. He even misspelled words he knew how to spell. Avi's papers often came back covered in red correction marks. His teachers thought he was just sloppy and not paying attention.

Soon, Avi grew to hate his Friday spelling tests. Worst of all, his sister, Emily, was very good at spelling. And, she was in Avi's class. After the seventh grade, Avi asked to be placed in a different class than Emily. Avi was good at science. So, he moved to the class of a popular science teacher.

Years later, Avi would learn why he has so much trouble writing. He has **dysgraphia**. He also learned that his parents had known about his condition. However, no one in the family had ever spoken of it.

Public School 8 is also called the Robert Fulton School. Robert Fulton worked to perfect the steam-powered boat.

High School Hiccup

After graduating from eighth grade, Avi attended Stuyvesant High School in Manhattan. Courses at this all-boys school focused on science. Avi's brother, Henry, also went to school there.

Avi struggled at Stuyvesant. The school was crowded. So, the teachers could not pay attention to every student. Avi failed all of his classes.

Avi's parents transferred him to Elisabeth Irwin High School. There, he had more time with his teachers. In addition, the school emphasized reading and writing.

However, Avi still had trouble with writing. Over time, many of his teachers gave up on trying to help him. Yet, one suggested Avi work with a writing **tutor**.

Avi took this advice. He began working with Ella Ratner. Ratner realized Avi had no problem coming up with stories. She also saw that he had interesting ideas. Ratner helped Avi work on his spelling and writing skills.

Until 1664, New York City was New Amsterdam, a Dutch settlement. Stuyvesant High School is named after Peter Stuyvesant, New Amsterdam's last governor.

Ratner was the first person to encourage Avi to write. He began to ignore the red correction marks that covered his schoolwork. He focused on writing plays and a journal.

In March 1955, Avi made an important declaration in his journal. He wrote, "I can't wait anymore. I'm going to become a **playwright**."

Playwright in Training

Avi graduated from high school in 1955. That fall, he enrolled in Antioch College in Yellow Springs, Ohio. He studied **playwriting**.

Antioch was a different kind of college. The classes were not structured like those at other schools. This learning **environment** did not work for Avi. He transferred to the University of Wisconsin in Madison, Wisconsin. There, he studied history and theater.

Avi spent nearly five years at the University of Wisconsin. In his senior year, he entered a play in the school's annual playwriting contest. Unfortunately, the contest judge thought English was not Avi's native language. Avi was **frustrated**, but he entered another play the next year.

This time, Avi's play won the contest! The play was staged at the university's theater. Inspired, Avi moved to San

Francisco, California, to become a **playwright**. There, he got a job with a theater. But after a year of hard work, none of his plays had been staged. **Frustrated** once again, he moved back to New York City.

Antioch Hall (right) was designed by James Renwick Jr. Renwick also designed the Smithsonian Institution's first building, known as the Castle.

Settling Down

Back in New York, Avi continued to write plays. He took odd jobs to earn money. While working as an acting coach, he met a woman named Joan Gabriner. Joan and Avi fell in love. They began talking about marriage.

Avi needed a better job if he was going to settle down. One day, he saw a job posting at the New York Public Library. The library's theater collection needed a clerk. Avi got the job!

Avi wanted to advance in the library system. So, he entered Columbia University to earn a master's **degree** in library science. For three years, Avi took classes at night and worked during the day. When he could spare some time, he continued to write plays.

In 1963, Avi and Joan were married. Their son Shaun was born in 1966. A friend told Avi he could make extra money illustrating children's books. Avi had always enjoyed drawing. So, he did some illustrations for a book and sent it to an editor.

*Opposite page: **Each year, the Pulitzer Prizes are awarded in Columbia University's Low Memorial Library.***

The editor liked Avi's drawings. She asked Avi to write his own book. Avi and his family were preparing to spend a year in England. He had just seven days before he left the country. What could he write in such a short time?

Sometimes Shaun asked Avi for a story about something, such as a glass of water. Avi would make up a story on the spot. The stories he had made up for Shaun became his first book. *Things That Sometimes Happen* was published in 1970.

A Writer at Last

Things That Sometimes Happen was a turning point for Avi. He had written plays and stories. Avi now realized his gifts lay in writing for kids.

While living in England, Avi and Joan welcomed another son, Kevin. Avi decided that having two kids meant he needed a better job. Back in the United States, Avi got a new job as a librarian at Trenton State College in Ewing, New Jersey.

While at his new job, Avi continued writing. He published his first novel for children in 1975. It is called *No More Magic.* Avi realized he was more comfortable writing novels than stories. In 1981, he published *A Place Called Ugly.* It was his first novel for young adults.

In 1982, Avi and Joan divorced. Avi's sister, Emily, introduced him to a friend of hers named Coppélia Kahn. It seemed like a perfect match. Coppélia was also recently divorced. She taught literature at a college. The two began spending a lot of time together.

Coppélia decided to take a job teaching at Brown University in Providence, Rhode Island. Avi and Coppélia married and moved to Providence. There, Avi decided against taking another library job. He wanted to earn a living as a full-time writer.

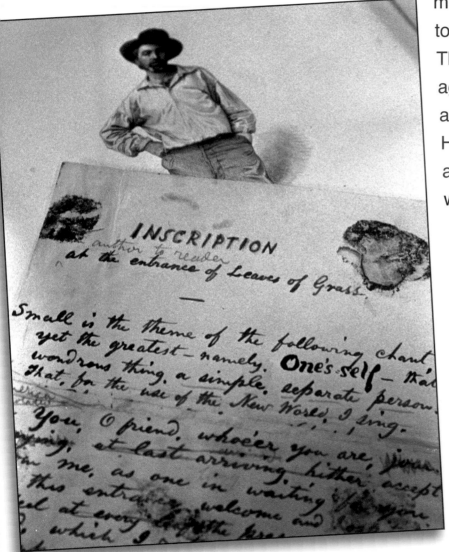

Trenton State College is now The College of New Jersey. The college's library holds the first copy of Walt Whitman's book Leaves of Grass. The book contains an introduction written in Whitman's own hand.

Honors and Awards

Avi dived into his writing career. In Providence, he was surrounded by history. In fact, the house Avi and Coppélia lived in became the setting for one of his novels.

Something Upstairs is about a boy who discovers the ghost of a murdered slave in his new house. The boy travels back in time to solve the crime.

Many of Avi's novels for young people have historical themes. *The Fighting Ground* was published in 1984. It is the story of a boy in the **American Revolution**. Avi's book shows clearly that war is not glamorous. *The Fighting Ground* earned Avi the **Scott O'Dell Award**.

In 1990, Avi wrote *The True Confessions of Charlotte Doyle*. It is about a girl from Providence who witnesses a **mutiny** on a ship. The voyage changes her and how she views her place in the world. To survive, she must question the values of the adults around her.

Opposite page: Providence has played an important role in U.S. history. University Hall at Brown University was used as a hospital during the American Revolution.

This part of Charlotte's character bothered some readers. Yet others praised the book. It was named a **Newbery Honor Book**.

The following year, Avi wrote another book that earned a Newbery Honor. In *Nothing But The Truth*, a student gets in trouble for humming along with the national anthem. His actions have wide-ranging, unintended consequences.

New Directions

In 1996, Avi moved in a new creative direction. Coppélia and Avi had divorced, and he had moved to Colorado. One night, a pair of raccoons gave Avi a story idea. He wrote *Keep Your Eye on Amanda* in 21 **installments**. The story ran in two local newspapers.

Soon, more than 400 newspapers were running Avi's **serial** stories. Avi hired other authors and illustrators to help him. He and his new wife, Linda Wright, created The Breakfast Serials company to manage the project.

Still, Avi continued to write novels. One day, he was listening to a book on tape about the Middle Ages. The author said that a **serf** could earn his freedom if he could escape to a free city and live there for a year and a day.

The comment got Avi thinking. The result was *Crispin: The Cross of Lead*. It is the story of a boy in 1377, who runs away from home. Eventually, he gains his freedom and learns more about himself. In 2003, *Crispin: The Cross of Lead* won the **Newbery Medal**. It was Avi's fiftieth book.

Avi signs copies of **Crispin: At the Edge Of the World**

In 2006, Avi continued Crispin's story in *Crispin: At the Edge Of the World.* That same year, he and several other writers started Authors Readers Theatre. The group reads and acts out scenes from the members' books.

Avi's book *The Seer of Shadows* was published in 2008. The story tells of young photographer Horace Carpetine. He takes pictures of a ghost! Avi writes great books that readers of all ages can enjoy. Fans can't wait to see what direction he will take next!

Glossary

activism - a practice that emphasizes direct action in support of or in opposition to a controversial issue. A person who practices activism is called an activist.

American Revolution - from 1775 to 1783. A war for independence between Great Britain and its North American colonies. The colonists won and created the United States of America.

complex - having many parts, details, ideas, or functions.

degree - a title given by a college to its graduates after they have completed their studies.

dysgraphia (dihs-GRAF-ee-uh) - impairment of the ability to write, usually caused by brain dysfunction or disease.

environment - the circumstances, objects, or conditions by which one is surrounded.

frustrated - having a sense of insecurity or dissatisfaction from unresolved problems or unfulfilled needs.

installment - part of a serial story.

mutiny - open rebellion against lawful authority, especially by sailors or soldiers against their officers.

Newbery Medal - an award given by the American Library Association to the author of the year's best children's book. Runners-up are called Newbery Honor Books.

playwright - a person who writes plays. Playwriting is the act of writing plays.

psychiatrist - a doctor who specializes in identifying and treating mental, emotional, and behavioral disorders.

Scott O'Dell Award - an annual award given by the O'Dell Award Committee to the author of an outstanding historical fiction book intended for children or young people.

serf - peasants bound to the land.

serial - an artistic work that appears in parts at certain intervals. Each part often ends in an exciting twist. The audience must wait until the next part appears to find out what happens next.

social work - providing organized public or private social services for the assistance of disadvantaged groups. A person who does social work is called a social worker.

tutor - to teach a student privately. The teacher is also called a tutor.

World War II - from 1939 to 1945, fought in Europe, Asia, and Africa. Great Britain, France, the United States, the Soviet Union, and their allies were on one side. Germany, Italy, Japan, and their allies were on the other side.

Web Sites

To learn more about Avi, visit ABDO Publishing Company on the World Wide Web at **www.abdopublishing.com**. Web sites about Avi are featured on our Book Links page. These links are routinely monitored and updated to provide the most current information available.

Index